# Counting Coup

**Leni Donlan**

Raintree

**Chicago, Illinois**

Designed by Michelle Lisseter, Kim Miracle,
and Bigtop
Printed in China

11 10 09 08 07
10 9 8 7 6 5 4 3 2 1

**Library of Congress
Cataloging-in-Publication Data**
   Library of Congress Cataloging-in-Publication Data

Donlan, Leni.
   Counting coup : customs of the Crow Nation / Leni
Donlan.
       p. cm. -- (American history through primary
sources)
   Includes bibliographical references and index.
   ISBN 1-4109-2421-1 (hc) -- ISBN 1-4109-2432-7 (pb)
   1. Crow Indians--Social life and customs--Juvenile
literature. 2. Crow
Indians--History--Juvenile literature. I. Title. II.
Series.

   E99.C92D66 2007
   305.897'5272--dc22
                                        2006008527

13-digit ISBNs
978-1-4109-2421-6 (hardcover)
978-1-4109-2432-2 (paperback)

**Acknowledgments**
The author and publisher are grateful to the
following for permission to reproduce copyright
material: Denver Public Library, Western History
Collection **pp. 7** (R. Throssel, X-31211), **14** (X-
31269), **15** (R. Throssel, X-31203), **17** (X-33702), **24**
(Nate Salsbury, NS-285), **25** (X-32085), **27** (D.F. Barry,
B-801); Library of Congress Prints and Photographs
Division **pp. 6**, **8**, **11**, **12–13**, **16**, **19**, **28**, **29**;
McCormick Library of Special Collections,
Northwestern University Library **pp. 9**, **20**, **21**, **23**.

Cover photograph of Chief Plenty Coup reproduced
with permission of Denver Public Library, Western
History Collection (D.F. Barry, B-801).

Photo research by Tracy Cummins.

Illustrations by Darren Lingard.

The publishers would like to thank Nancy Harris,
Joy Rogers, George Reed, Jr., and Isabel Tovar for their
assistance in the preparation of this book.

Every effort has been made to contact copyright
holders of any material reproduced in this book. Any
omissions will be rectified in subsequent printings if
notice is given to the publishers.

**Disclaimer**
All the Internet addresses (URLs) given in this book
were valid at the time of going to press. However, due
to the dynamic nature of the Internet, some addresses
may have changed, or sites may have changed or
ceased to exist since publication. While the author and
publishers regret any inconvenience this may cause
readers, no responsibility for any such changes can be
accepted by either the author or the publishers.

It is recommended that adults supervise children on
the Internet.

# Contents

Some words are printed in bold, **like this**. You can find out what they mean on page 30. You can also look in the box at the bottom of the page where they first appear.

# Before The White Man Came

Native Americans have been in North America for thousands of years. Some people believe they came to North America over a land bridge (see map). Other people believe that Native Americans have always been in North America.

Native Americans lived off the land for thousands of years. They were fishermen and hunters. They ate nuts and berries. They ate plants that grew under the ground. They trapped animals. They ate the animals' meat. They used the animals' fur for clothing.

Some Native Americans became farmers. They stayed in one place. Other Native Americans moved from place to place. They followed the animals they hunted. People who move from place to place to find food are called **nomads**.

Many European explorers came to North America in the 1500s. They found Native Americans living all across the land.

**nomad**   person who does not live in one place, but rather moves from place to place in search of food

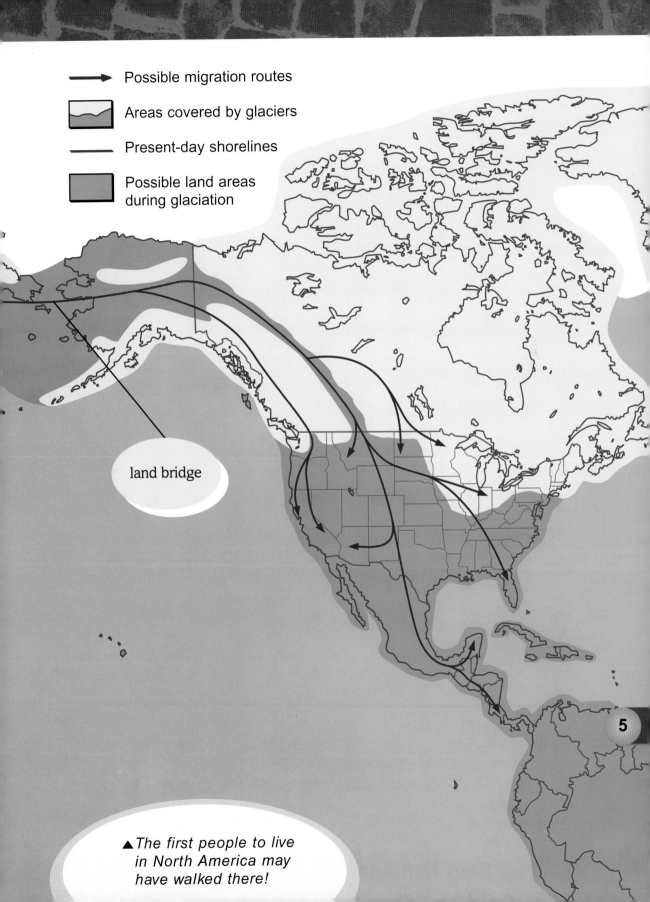

Possible migration routes

Areas covered by glaciers

Present-day shorelines

Possible land areas during glaciation

land bridge

▲ *The first people to live in North America may have walked there!*

# The Crow Nation

In the 1500s, groups of Native American people settled around the Big Horn Mountains. These mountains are in the northwestern United States. These people were known as the Apsaalooke. They hunted **bison**. The whole **tribe** (group) was too big to move together. So, they divided into four **bands** (small groups).

The Apsaalooke bands lived on different parts of the Big Horn Mountains. They all spoke the same language. They told the same stories. The bands often visited each other. The whole tribe did not come together often, though.

These Native ▲ Americans are hunting bison.

The name *Apsaalooke* means "Children of the Long-Beaked Bird." European **settlers** later changed the tribe name to Crow. These settlers had moved to the northwestern United States. Settlers are people who live in a new place.

## Different names

*The four Apsaalooke bands each had a different name:*
- *The Mountain Crows*
- *The River Crows*
- *The Kicked in the Belly*
- *The Beaver Dried Fur.*

▼ *This is the home of the River Crow in Montana.*

| band | small group of people from a large tribe who live and travel together |
| --- | --- |
| bison | large, brown, shaggy-haired animal |
| settler | person who moves to or lives in a new place |
| tribe | large group of people who have common family backgrounds |

# Counting Coup—The Warriors

Chiefs were the leaders of a **tribe**. To become a chief, a man proved himself. He had to prove he was a good **warrior**. A warrior is a fighter. He proved this by:

- leading a successful fight against an enemy;
- capturing an enemy's horse;
- being the first to touch an enemy in battle;
- getting an enemy's weapon.

▲ *These Native Americans wait for an attack signal from their leader.*

| | |
|---|---|
| **coup** | honor earned through success in a battle or contest |
| **coup-stick** | decorated wooden stick that showed a warrior s coup (honors) |
| **warrior** | experienced fighter in battle or war |

Warriors earned **coup** (honors). The more dangerous an action was, the more coup a warrior earned. Fighting in close contact or by hand earned coup. Snatching an enemy's weapon earned coup. Getting an enemy's horses earned coup.

Some warriors carried wooden sticks. They were called **coup-sticks**. They showed how many coup they had earned.

Medicine Crow has three ▶ animal tails hanging from his coup-stick. They show that he earned three coup.

9

# Clan and Family

Every person in a **tribe** belonged to a **clan**. A clan is a group of related families. These families helped each other.

Girls married at a very young age. A girl's family picked a husband for her. Then the married couple joined the woman's family. Their children became part of the mother's clan.

The mother's brothers taught the boys how to dress. They taught them how to ride horses. They taught them how to hunt and make weapons. The mother and older sisters taught girls how to behave. They taught them how to dress and cook. The girls learned to scrape **bison hides** (skins) and prepare bison meat.

The **elders** were the older members of the clan. They taught the children about their history and traditions.

## Family names

*Crow children called their father's brothers "father," not "uncle." They called their mother's sisters "mother," not "aunt." They called their mother's brothers "big brother," not "uncle."*

**clan**  group of related families within a tribe who help one another

▼ *This woman is holding her baby in a **cradleboard**. It prevents the baby from crawling away.*

# Hunting Bison

Hunting **bison** was very important to the Crow. The Crow ate the bison's meat. They used bison **hide** (skin) to make homes. The homes were called **tepees**. Tepees are cone-shaped tents. They used bison hide to make clothes and warm blankets. They used bison bones to make needles and tools.

The Crow had great respect for bison. The hunters said a prayer before each bison hunt. They thanked the bison for giving up its life for them.

**stampede**   when animals run in a panic
**tepee**       cone-shaped tent made from bison skin

The Crow hunted bison without guns. They would make the bison **stampede**. A stampede is when animals run in a frightened rush. Then the Crow chased the bison over a cliff.

The Crow carried the bison meat back to camp. They ate the fresh bison meat. The Crow women dried the rest of the meat. Then the **clan** could eat the meat during the winter months.

▼ *These hunters are looking for bison.*

# Life in a Crow Camp

The Crow lived in **tepees** (tents). Each teepee had a frame. The frame was made of 21 long poles. The poles were covered with **bison hides** (skins). A tepee was open at the top. Smoke could escape from the fire at the tepee's center. Families slept on beds along the sides of the tepee.

▼ This is a Crow camp. Can you see the long poles that hold up the tepees?

| | |
|---|---|
| **breechcloth** | light animal skins worn by men in the warm summer months |
| **moccasin** | soft leather shoes often decorated with beadwork |

It was hot in the summer. The men wore only **breechcloths**. The breechcloths were made from animal skins. They hung from their waists in front and back. They wore soft, slipper-like shoes. They were called **moccasins**. In cool weather, men wore shirts and pants. These were made from animal skins. Women wore long dresses all year round. These were made of animal skins, too.

In the winter, men and women wore coats made from bison hides. They wore fur on the inside for extra warmth and softness.

# Crow women

Crow women were busy. They gathered food. They scraped **bison hides** (skins). They stretched them out to dry. The women cooked and sewed. They cared for the children. When the Crow moved, the women took down and set up the **tepees** (tents).

Women made **travois**. These are carts for carrying things. Dogs or horses pulled loaded travois when camp was moved. Travois were also sometimes used to carry children and **elders** (older people).

▼ *This Crow woman is stretching an animal skin. The Crow people used the skins for clothing.*

**elk**       large animal that looks a lot like a deer
**travois**   cart used by hunters

The Crow women were famous for decorating their clothes. They made beautiful designs. They often used the teeth of **elk** (deer-like animals) to decorate clothing. They also used beads. Sometimes they used feathers, seeds, and seashells.

Crow children had to help with chores. But there was also time for games, swimming, and fun.

▼ *Crow women were in charge of moving the camp.*

# Traditions and Ceremonies

The Crow **elders** (older people) told stories. This was important. It was how the adults and children learned their history. They learned about their **clan** (family group). They learned about their **tribe** (larger group). They also learned about their past from pictures.

The Crow used pictures to keep records of events. They recorded things such as **bison** hunts. A picture could show how many bison were killed in a hunt. They could also show battles in pictures. Pictures could record all the special things that happened to a clan or tribe.

The Crow often carved these pictures into the walls of caves. Sometimes they painted the pictures onto animal skins.

Traders and soldiers gave the Crow drawing materials. The Crow made pictures on paper. They used watercolors, pens, and pencils. Their pictures showed hunters. They showed **warriors** and dancers.

▼ *The Crow listen as a story is told.*

19

# Ceremonies

The Crow believed that the gods spoke to them in **visions** (dreams). In a vision, a spirit talked. The spirit might take the form of an animal. It might be a **bison**, bear, or eagle. The visions helped to guide the lives of the Crow people.

The Sun Dance was an important Crow ceremony. The Crow would fast. Fasting means not eating or drinking. They would pray and dance. They did this for many days. The Crow often had visions during the Sun Dance.

This Crow Sun ▶ Dancer is wearing a **breechcloth**.

**vision** ideas and thoughts that a person has

◀ *The Crow would fast and pray during the Sun Dance.*

The Crow held another ceremony when they planted tobacco. Tobacco was believed to be a special gift from the gods.

The Crow were not afraid of death. When Crow died, their bodies were put high off the ground. This kept the bodies safe from animals. The Crow also believed that this height made the dead closer to the gods.

# After The White Man Came

In the 1700s, fur traders came to the Crow lands. They wanted the Crow to help them. They wanted help finding animals with fur coats. The traders killed the animals. They sold the furs to other **settlers**. They gave the Native Americans items to pay for the fur. They gave them things like blankets and beads.

Sadly, these fur traders also gave the Native Americans many new diseases. In the 1700s, thousands of Native Americans died from these diseases.

In the 1800s, settlers traveled through Crow lands. They came in covered wagons. They were searching for land where they could start a new life. The Crow did not want to give up their land. They saw the settlers as their enemies.

These settlers taught the Crow new skills. They gave the Native Americans new customs and ideas. But the settlers also changed the Crow forever.

▼ The **warrior** on the left wears a coat of heavy blanket material. Traders gave coats like this to the Crow.

23

## Crow scouts

In the 1800s, some Crow joined the U.S. Army. They were good scouts. They helped U.S. soldiers plan battles.

# Educating Crow Children

The Crow knew that education was important. The whole **clan** (family group) taught the children. They taught them about their history.

In the late 1800s, the U.S. government thought Native Americans should give up their ways. They thought Native Americans should act like the **settlers**. So, the U.S. government started special schools. The schools were for Native American children. They taught them how to be like the children of settlers.

▼ This is a Native American boarding school. It is in Pine Ridge, South Dakota.

By 1893 Native American parents were forced to send their children to these special schools. The children often lived at the school. They did not see their families for months. These students could only speak English at school. They could not practice any of their traditions. They wore uniforms. They had their hair cut.

This was a very unhappy time in the life of the Crow. By the 1920s, these schools were no longer required.

◀ This photo shows three Native American students. It was taken at the Carlisle Native American School in Carlisle, Pennsylvania.

# Chief Plenty Coup's Vision

A young Crow named Plenty Coup had a **vision** (dream).
He saw a herd of **bison**. The bison disappeared.
He saw an old man. The old man was himself, years later.
He saw a violent storm. The storm destroyed a forest.

Plenty Coup spoke with the **tribe elders** about his vision.
The elders said the vision meant:

- **Settlers** would move onto Crow land.
- All the bison would be gone.
- The Crow land would be taken away.

Plenty Coup's vision was true. By 1880 the Crow had lost much of their land. The bison were gone. The Crow were moved to a **reservation** in Montana. A reservation is an area of public land reserved for special use.

Today, the Crow still live on the reservation. Many Crow still belong to a **clan** (family group). They still respect their elders. They teach their children Crow traditions. But Crow life has changed forever.

**reservation**   area of public land reserved for special use

▼ In 1904 Chief Plenty Coup became the last chief of the Crow Nation. He worked to protect his people and the Crow land.

# Chief Plenty Coup Honors Other Warriors

The Tomb of the Unknown Soldier is in Arlington National Cometery. The cemetery is near Washington, D.C. It represents soldiers who died in war, but whose bodies could not be identified.

On November 11, 1921, Chief Plenty Coup attended a ceremony at the Tomb of the Unknown Soldier. He represented all Native Americans. Chief Plenty Coup gave a speech at the ceremony. He left gifts on the tomb. Two of those gifts were a **warbonnet** and a **coup-stick**.

▼ *This is the Tomb of the Unknown Soldier. It is in Arlington National Cemetery.*

**warbonnet**   long feathered ceremonial headdress

This is Chief Plenty ▲ Coup, the last of the Crow chiefs.

This is Chief Plenty Coup's speech, in English:

*I am told that this soldier is one who is known only to God…*
*Because of the honors given to him by all of the countries that*
*were in the war, he truly is a chief. I hope that the Great Spirit*
*will grant that these noble* **warriors** *have not given up their*
*lives in vain [for no reason] and that there will be peace to all*
*men hereafter. This is the Native Americans' hope and prayer.*

29

# Glossary

**band** small group of people from a large tribe who live and travel together

**bison** large, brown, shaggy-haired animal

**breechcloth** light animal skins worn by men in the warm summer months

**clan** group of related families within a tribe who help one another

**coup** honor earned through success in a battle or a contest

**coup-stick** decorated wooden stick that showed a warrior's coup (honors)

**cradleboard** board to which a baby is strapped to keep it from crawling away into harm

**elder** wise older person

**elk** large animal that looks a lot like a deer

**moccasin** soft leather shoe, often decorated with beadwork

**nomad** person who does not live in one place, but rather moves from place to place in search of food

**reservation** area of public land reserved for special use

**settler** person who moves to or lives in a new place

**stampede** when animals run in a panic

**tepee** cone-shaped tent made from bison skin

**travois** cart used by hunters

**tribe** large group of people who have common family backgrounds

**vision** ideas and thoughts that a person has when he or she is in a dream-like state

**warbonnet** long feathered ceremonial headdress

**warrior** experienced fighter in battle or war

# Want to Know More?

## Books to read

- Tarbescu, Edith. *The Crow.* New York: Franklin Watts, 2000.
- Maher, Erin. *Traditions of the Crow People.* New York: Rosen Publishing Group, 2003.

## Websites

- http://www.nativeamericans.com Visit this site to find out more about the history of Native American tribes.
- http://www.crownations.net Learn more about Crow celebrations and history at this site.

Read **Rebirth of a People: Harlem Renaissance** to find out about the many talented writers, painters, and other artists of the Harlem Renaissance.

Read **When Will I Get In?: Segregation and Civil Rights** to find out about the struggle against segregation and Jim Crow laws.

# Index